FRESH DESIGNS
SCARVES

FEATURING DESIGNS BY

Amy Duncan
Claire Valentine
Daniel Yuhas
Hannah Cuviello
Heather Keiser
Jenny Williams
Jill Wright
Margarete Dolff
Sylvia Cannizzaro
Valeria Kerkkä

AND PHOTOGRAPHY BY

Robert Gladys / Fractured Photography

COOPERATIVE PRESS
Cleveland, OH
cooperativepress.com

FRESH DESIGNS: SCARVES

Library of Congress Control Number: 2011912388
ISBN 13: 978-0-9792017-8-3
First Edition
Published by Cooperative Press
http://www.cooperativepress.com

Patterns © 2011, their designers, as credited
Photos © 2011, Robert Gladys, Fractured Photography (fracturedphotography.com), except Avonleigh Scarf, page 20.

Makeup by Elle Gemma, Spell Cosmetics (spellcosmetics.com)
Models: Arabella Proffer, Elle Gemma, Rachel Harner, Susan Prahst, Terra Incognita

Every effort has been made to ensure that all the information in this book is accurate at the time of publication, however Cooperative Press neither endorses nor guarantees the content of external links referenced in this book.

If you have questions or comments about this book, or need information about licensing, custom editions, special sales, or academic/corporate purchases, please contact Cooperative Press: info@cooperativepress.com or 13000 Athens Ave C288, Lakewood, OH 44107 USA

No part of this book may be reproduced in any form, except brief excerpts for the purpose of review, without prior written permission of the publisher. Thank you for respecting our copyright.

FOR COOPERATIVE PRESS

Senior Editor: Shannon Okey
Assistant Editor: Elizabeth Green Musselman
Developmental Editor: Abra Forman
Technical Editor: Alexandra Virgiel
Production Manager: MJ Kim
With additional assistance by Sarah Jo Mosbeck

TABLE OF CONTENTS

AMY DUNCAN	Majere	(page 5)
CLAIRE VALENTINE	Monkey Puzzle Scarf	(page 9)
DANIEL YUHAS	Shaker Moebius	(page 13)
HANNAH CUVIELLO	Scarf Scarf Revolution	(page 15)
HEATHER KEISER	Scrunchy Scarf	(page 19)
JENNY WILLIAMS	Avonleigh Scarf/Hood	(page 21)
JILL WRIGHT	Spanish Steppes	(page 25)
MARGARETE DOLFF	Tossed Leaves Scarf	(page 29)
SYLVIA CANNIZZARO	Diamond Sampler	(page 33)
VALERIA KERKKÄ	Laineet	(page 41)
ACKNOWLEDGMENTS		(page 43)
ABOUT COOPERATIVE PRESS AND THE FRESH DESIGNS SERIES		(page 46)

MAJERE
BY AMY DUNCAN

INTERMEDIATE

Mysterious dark wandering cables interspersed with light wielding dropped stitches. Elegant warmth with a vampiric punk edge for the light and dark in us all. Winter doesn't stand a chance.

FINISHED MEASUREMENTS

Width: 11"/22cm
Length: 48"/122cm

MATERIALS

Indigodragonfly MCN Worsted [80% merino wool, 10% cashmere, 10% nylon; 180yd/165m per 100g skein]; color Goth to a Flame; 4 skeins

1 set US #10.5/6.5mm straight needles

6 stitch markers
Cable needle (cn)

GAUGE

14 sts/16rows = 4"/10cm in stockinette with yarn doubled

CHART

See page 6

PATTERN

With 2 strands of yarn held together, cast on 40 sts.

Set-up section:
Row 1 [RS]: Knit.
Row 2: K7, pm, (k1, yo, k1, pm, k10, pm) twice, k1, yo, k1, pm, k7. 43 sts.

Work the 16 rows of Chart 12 times, or to desired length.

Ending section:
Row 1 [RS]: K7, p1, drop next stitch, (p1, k10, p1, drop next stitch) twice, p1, k7. 40 sts.
Row 2: Knit.
Bind off.

FINISHING

With a firm but gentle hand, work the dropped stitches down to the bottom.

Block to desired dimensions and drape.

ABOUT THE DESIGNER

Amy Duncan began knitting in 2007, and soon the dining room was covered in yarns, patterns, and blocking squares. You can find her at http://www.TwoSticksandaSheep.com and on Ravelry and Twitter as Duncks.

http://www.twosticksandasheep.com
Duncks on Ravelry.com

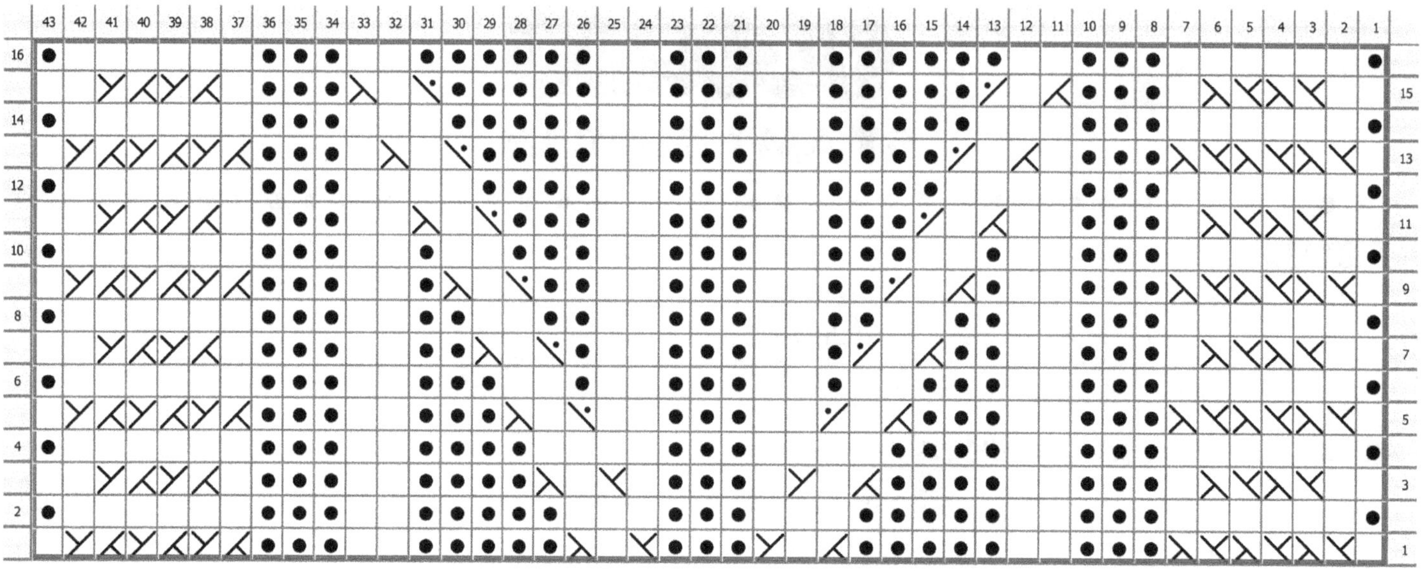
43 42 41 40 39 38 37 36 35 34 33 32 31 30 29 28 27 26 25 24 23 22 21 20 19 18 17 16 15 14 13 12 11 10 9 8 7 6 5 4 3 2 1
16
14
12
10
8
6
4
2
15
13
11
9
7
5
3
1

MONKEY PUZZLE SCARF

BY CLAIRE VALENTINE

BEGINNER

The Monkey Puzzle scarf was inspired by the ladder like arrangement of branches of the Monkey Puzzle tree, reproduced here in simple knit and purl stitches. It is a cozy scarf to keep you warm in cold weather.

FINISHED MEASUREMENTS

Width: 9"/23cm
Length: 71"/180cm

MATERIALS

Natural Born Dyers Falkland Chunky [100% Falkland wool; 120yds/109m per 100g skein]; color blues and greens (OOAK); 3 skeins

1 set US #10.5/6.5mm straight needles

GAUGE

13 sts/16 rows = 4"/10cm in stockinette

CHART

See page 10

STITCH INSTRUCTIONS

Monkey Puzzle Pattern
Rows 1–4: Sl1 wyif, k17, p12, k3.
Rows 5–8: Sl1 wyif, k2, p12, k18.
Rep Rows 1–8.

PATTERN

Cast on 33 sts.
Knit 6 rows, slipping the first st of every row wyif.
Work Monkey Puzzle patt following written instructions or chart until scarf measures approx. 69.5"/176cm, or 1.5"/4cm less than desired length.
Knit 6 rows, slipping the first st of every row wyif.
Bind off loosely knitwise.

FINISHING

Weave in ends.

Blocking is not essential; however it will even out the stitches and give a more professional finish to the scarf. To block, soak the scarf in lukewarm water without agitation for 15–20 minutes. Gently squeeze the excess water from the scarf (rolling the scarf in an old towel helps here) then pin the scarf out to size, taking care to keep the edges straight and the corners square. Allow to air dry.

ABOUT THE DESIGNER

Claire lives in Newcastle upon Tyne in the UK with her partner, cat and too many fish to count. She has been knitting for a number of years, and has recently started to design items. She can be found on Ravelry as Panperoxide.

http://panperoxide.blogspot.com
Panperoxide on Ravelry.com

	33	32	31	30	29	28	27	26	25	24	23	22	21	20	19	18	17	16	15	14	13	12	11	10	9	8	7	6	5	4	3	2	1	
8	V	•	•													•	•	•	•	•	•	•	•	•	•	•	•	•	•	•	•	•	•	
																			•	•	•	•	•	•	•	•	•	•	•	•	•	•	V	7
6	V	•	•													•	•	•	•	•	•	•	•	•	•	•	•	•	•	•	•	•	•	
																			•	•	•	•	•	•	•	•	•	•	•	•	•	•	V	5
4	V	•	•	•	•	•	•	•	•	•	•	•	•	•	•	•															•	•	•	
			•	•	•	•	•	•	•	•	•	•	•	•	•																		V	3
2	V	•	•		•	•	•	•	•	•	•	•	•	•	•																•	•	•	
				•	•	•	•	•	•	•	•	•	•	•	•																		V	1

SHAKER MOEBIUS

BY DANIEL YUHAS

INTERMEDIATE

Shaker rib, or brioche, is a deeply textured ribbing that's made without ever needing to purl. This simple scarf is knit 'til it's just long enough, then seamed into a moebius.

FINISHED MEASUREMENTS

Measured as a moebius, 5.5"/14cm wide, infinitely long.
Measured as a rectangle before seaming, 5.5"/14cm wide x 25"/63cm long.

MATERIALS

Berroco Jasper [100% merino wool; 98yd/90m per 50g skein]; color AstraBerry (3847); 2 skeins

1 set US #9/5.5mm straight needles

Crochet hook for provisional cast on
Waste yarn

GAUGE

16 sts = 4"/10cm in shaker rib
18 sts/22 rows = 4"/10cm in stockinette

PATTERN NOTES

Beginning with a provisional cast on, this piece is worked straight like a regular scarf, then seamed into a moebius shape.

STITCH INSTRUCTIONS

Crochet Provisional Cast On

With waste yarn, make a chain the number of sts you need to cast on. Fasten off. Tie a knot in the tail so you know which end to unravel from, later.

With knitting needle and main yarn, pick up and knit 1 st in each "bump" along the backside of the chain.

To unzip the cast on later, find the end with the knotted tail, pick out the fastened-off chain, and pull on the tail to unravel.

PATTERN

Cast on 22 stitches using crochet provisional method.
Row 1: [WS] Knit.
Row 2: Sl2, k1, *yo, sl1 pwise wyib, k1; rep from * to last 3 sts, k3. 30 sts.
Row 3: Sl2 pwise wyib, k1, *yo, sl1 pwise wyib, knit next st tog with yo; rep from * to last 3 sts, p3.
Row 4: Sl2 pwise wyib, k1, *yo, sl1 pwise wyib, knit next st tog with yo; rep from * to last 3 sts, k3.
Repeat Rows 3–4 until scarf measures 25"/63cm, ending with Row 3.

Next row [RS]: Sl2 pwise wyib, k1, *p1, knit next st tog with yo; rep from * to last 3 sts, k3. 22 sts.
Next row: Knit.

FINISHING

Remove waste yarn from cast on and transfer live stitches to needle. Arrange scarf into moebius shape (i.e. a loop with a single bend in the fabric). Graft ends together with Kitchener stitch. Weave in ends.

ABOUT THE DESIGNER

I taught myself to knit during a break at college, fumbling over the illustrations in a teach-yourself book, and the obsession just keeps getting deeper as the years go by. My designs have appeared in books and magazines, and I've taught knitters new tricks at festivals and on the subway. It's pretty amazing how you can make just about anything you want with two sticks, some string, and two simple stitches. You can see more of my designs at www.Super-FunKnits.com.

SCARF SCARF REVOLUTION

BY HANNAH CUVIELLO

INTERMEDIATE

Inspired by the popular video dance game, this scarf consists of double-knit panels, each with an arrow pointing in a different direction. Each panel is picked up and knit off the edge of the previous panel.

FINISHED MEASUREMENTS

Each panel: 6.25"/15.5cm square
Total length: 72"/183cm

MATERIALS

[A] Yarn Love Charlotte Bronte-Worsted Weight [100% organic merino wool; 280yd/256m per 110g skein]; color Earl Grey; 2 skeins
[B] Yarn Love Charlotte Bronte-Worsted Weight; color Haute Couture; 2 skeins

1 set US #7/4.5mm straight needles

GAUGE

19 sts/28 rows = 4"/10cm in double knit stockinette

PATTERN NOTES

Picking up stitches in double knit pattern, you will always be picking up the B color knitwise and the A color purlwise.

Side A refers to the side with yarn A as the background color and B as the motif.

Side B refers to the side with yarn B as the background color and A as the motif.

STITCH INSTRUCTIONS

2-Color, Long-Tail Cast On
See page 17

2-Color Double Knitting

For an excellent online tutorial, refer to Alasdair Post Quinn's article in Twist Collective: http://tinyurl.com/double-knitting

If you'd like to explore double knitting further, check out his book *Extreme Double Knitting* (Cooperative Press, 2011).

CHART

See page 16

CHART KEY

Each charted square represents 2 stitches, one on the facing side of the work and one on the back side.
White squares: On Side A, k1 with A, p1 with B; on Side B, k1 with B, p1 with A.
Shaded squares: On Side A, k1 with B, p1 with A; on Side B, k1 with A, p1 with B.

PATTERN

First Panel
Using 2-Color Long Tail Cast On, cast on 56 sts (28 pairs of A and B). Begin working chart in double knitting; first row is Side A. Work through Row 42, turn and bind off on Side A in double knitting to the last stitch. Do not turn.

Second Panel

With A side facing, rotate the preceding panel one-quarter turn clockwise. The remaining stitch (should be color B) counts as 1. *Pick up one stitch of A purlwise, then one in B knitwise; repeat from * across the edge of the panel until you have 56 sts. Turn and begin working chart. First row will be Side B.

For third and fourth panels, work as Second Panel but with the chart upside down, beginning at Row 42 and working through Row 1. Bind off as before.

Repeat the process ad nauseum, ad infinitum, or until it is desired length, whichever comes first. Scarf shown has 14 panels.
Bind off all sts.

FINISHING

Weave in all ends and block.

ABOUT THE DESIGNER

Hannah Cuviello (hannahcuv on Ravelry) does not remember a time when yarn was not a huge part of her life. Lately, it has been even more so as she and her family run their online yarn store, Abundant Yarn Online (www.abundant-yarn.com).

http://www.abundant-yarn.com
hannahcuv on Ravelry.com

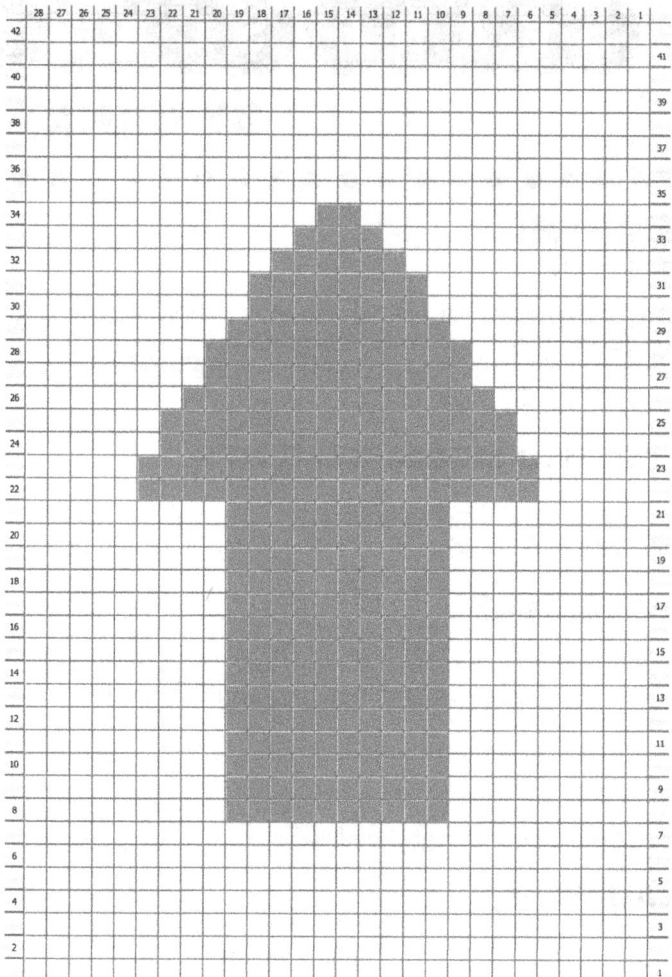

TWO-COLOR, LONG-TAIL CAST ON

1. Tie ends of A and B together, anchoring them with your finger.

5. Pick up strand of B and bring through A loop.

2. Insert tip of needle under B strand and over A strand, pulling back through B loop (basic long tail cast on)

6. One B stitch cast on.

3. One A stitch cast on

7. Continue until you have 28 pairs of stitches cast on (one of each color in a pair).

4. Insert tip of needle up through A loop from back to front.

SCRUNCHY SCARF
BY HEATHER KEISER

EASY

A gathered scarf that resembles a long stretched-out hair scrunchy. It is knit in the round with tassels on each end.

FINISHED MEASUREMENTS

Length: 54"/137cm, not including tassels

MATERIALS

Kangaroo Dyer Poet Seat [50% superwash merino, 50% silk; 437yd/399m per 100g skein]; color: Victorian Lilac; 4 skeins

1 set US #6/4mm double pointed needles OR 29"/74cm US #6/4mm circular needle using magic loop techniques

4 pieces scrap yarn
6 stitch markers, 3 each of two different colors (A and B)
1 stitch marker in a third color (C)

GAUGE

20 sts/28 rows = 4"/10cm in stockinette with two strands of yarn held together

PATTERN NOTES

This scarf was knit with two strands of yarn held together. Alternatively this scarf could be knit with a single strand of a worsted weight or heavier yarn.

PATTERN

With 2 strands of yarn held together, cast on 54 sts, leaving a tail about 15–20"/38–51cm long. Pm color C and join to work in the round. Tie a piece of scrap yarn at the join, and another after 27 sts. (These mark finishing points for later.)
Rnd 1: K6, pm color A, k7, pm color B, k1 tbl, k6, pm color A, k13, pm color B, k1 tbl, k6, pm color A, k7, pm color B, k1 tbl, k6.
Rnds 2–9: Knit.
Rnd 10: *Knit to A marker, sl marker, k1 tbl; rep from * twice more, knit to end.
Rnds 11–18: Knit.
Rnd 19: *Knit to B marker, sl marker, from wrong side pick up the twisted st 18 rows directly below next st, then knit it tog with next st; rep from * twice more, knit to end.
Rnd 20: *Knit to B marker, sl marker, k1 tbl; rep from * twice more, knit to end.
Rnds 21–28: Knit.
Rnd 29: *Knit to A marker, sl marker, from wrong side pick up the twisted st 18 rows directly below next st, then knit it tog with next st; rep from * twice more, knit to end.
Rnd 30: *Knit to A marker, sl marker, k1 tbl; rep from * twice more, knit to end.
Rnds 31–38: Knit.
Repeat Rnds 19–38 for 54"/137cm or desired length, ending with Rnd 19 or 29.
Knit 1 rnd.
Next rnd: Bind off 27 sts, tie a piece of scrap yarn around the work at this point, bind off rem 27 sts, tie another piece of scrap yarn. Leave a tail of yarn about 15–20"/38–51cm long.

FINISHING

Use the long tails to seam both ends of the scarf closed between the scrap yarn markers. Remove scrap yarn. Work tassels onto ends of scarf, if desired. Those on the scarf shown are about 5.5"/14cm long, and there are five on each end.

ABOUT THE DESIGNER

Heather C. Keiser; graphic designer by day, creative workaholic by night. Heather has over a decade of experience in the field. You can view her portfolio at www.keisergraphics.com. She is always busy on a multitude of projects, but there is always room for one more. Ravelry ID: hkeiser

http://www.keisergraphics.com/
hkeiser on Ravelry.com

AVONLEIGH SCARF / HOOD

BY JENNY WILLIAMS

INTERMEDIATE

A vine wanders back and forth across this scarf, accented by leaves and berries. The scarf is knit in two pieces and grafted together. A hood is then added to create a warm, dramatic accessory you'll love.

FINISHED MEASUREMENTS

Width: 5"/12.5cm
Length: 80"/203cm

MATERIALS

Alpaca with a Twist Baby Twist [100% Baby Alpaca; 549 yd per 250g skein]; color #3006 Lumberjack; 1 skein

US #5/3.75mm circular or straight needles
US #4/3.5mm circular or straight needles

Stitch holder
Cable needle (cn)
Tapestry needle

GAUGE

24 sts/29 rows = 4"/10cm in blocked stockinette using larger needles

STITCH INSTRUCTIONS

- C2F (Cable 2 Front) Sl 1 st to cn and hold at front of work, k1, k1 from cn
- C3F (Cable 3 Front) Sl 2 sts to cn and hold at front of work, p1 st, k2 from cn
- C4F (Cable 4 Front) Sl 2 sts to cn and hold at front of work, p 2 sts, k2 from cn
- C2B (Cable 2 Back) Sl 1 st to cn and hold at back of work, k1, k1 from cn
- C3B (Cable 3 Back) Sl 1 st to cn and hold at back of work, k2 sts, p1 from cn
- C4B (Cable 4 Back) Sl 2 sts to cn and hold at back of work, k2, p2 from cn
- MB (Make Bobble) P1, k1, p1, k1 into next st; turn, p4, turn, k4, turn, p4, turn, lift 2nd, 3rd, and 4th sts over 1st st; slip st to RH needle
- C4FMB (Cable 4 Front Make Bobble) Sl 2 sts to cn and hold at front of work, p1, MB, k2 from cn
- C4BMB (Cable 4 Back Make Bobble) Slip 2 sts to cn and hold at back of work, k2, sl2 sts from cn to LH needle, MB, p1
- T2F (Twist 2 Front) Sl 1 st to cn and hold at front of work, p1, k1 from cn
- T2B (Twist 2 Back) Sl 1 st to cn and hold at back of work, k1, p1 from cn

CHARTS

LACE CHART

	11	10	9	8	7	6	5	4	3	2	1	
14		●								●		
		●								●		13
12		●								●		
		●								●		11
10		●								●		
		●								●		9
8												
	\	O	/	O	/	O	/	O		O	/	7
6												
	\	B	O	/	O	/	O		O	B	/	5
4												
	\	B	B	O	/	O		O	B	B	/	3
2												
	\	B	B	B	O		O	B	B	B	/	1

LEAF CHART

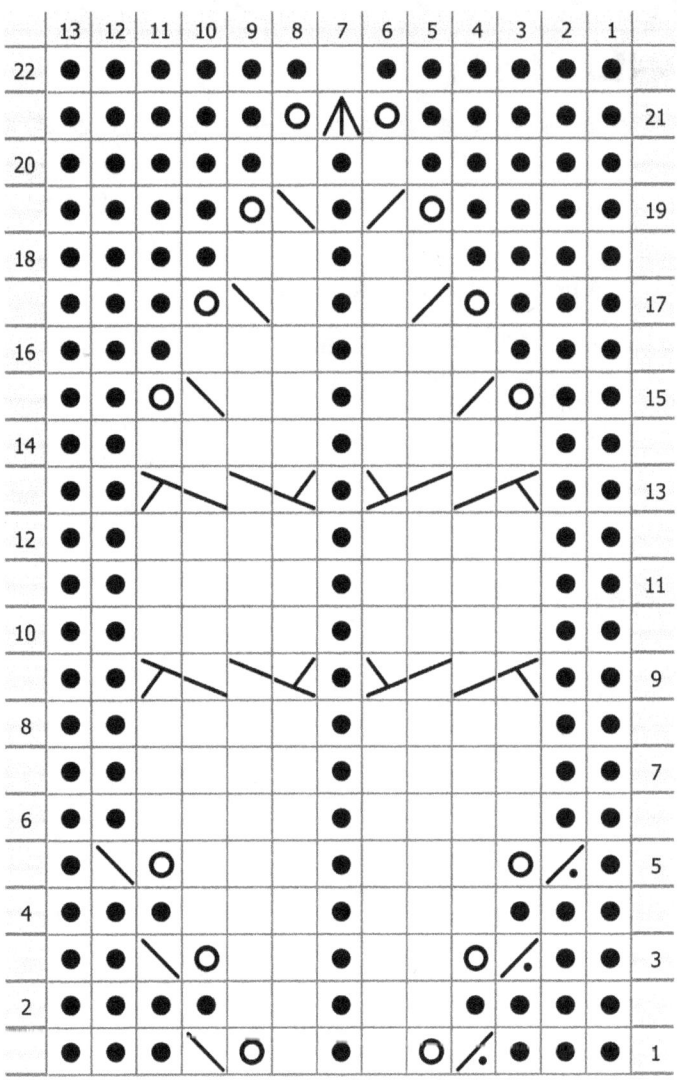

Row 17: K4, p5, k1, p1, k1, p18, k4.
Row 18: K22, p1, k1, p1, k9.

Leaf on Right
Row 19 [RS]: K4, work Leaf Chart over next 13 sts, p13, k4.
Row 20: K17, work Leaf Chart over 13 sts, k4.
Rows 21–40: Repeat Rows 19–20 until Leaf Chart is complete.

Vine Winding Left
Row 41 [RS]: K4, p6, C2F, purl to last 4 sts, k4.
All even rows 42–60 [WS]: K4, knit the knit sts and any bobble sts and purl the purl sts to last 4 sts, k4.
Row 43: K4, p6, C4F, p16, k4.
Row 45: K4, p8, C3F, p15, k4.
Row 47: K4, p9, C4F, p13, k4.
Row 49: K4, p11, C3F, p12, k4.
Row 51: K4, p12, C4F, p10, k4.
Row 53: K4, p14, C3F, MB, p8, k4.
Row 55: K4, p15, C3F, MB, p7, k4.
Row 57: K4, p16, C4FMB, p6, k4.
Row 59: K4, p18, k1, T2F, p5, k4.

Leaf on Left
Row 61 [RS]: K4, p13, work Leaf Chart over next 13 sts, k4.
Row 62: K4, work Leaf Chart over 13 sts, k17.
Rows 63–82: Repeat Rows 61–62 until Leaf Chart is complete.

Vine Winding Right
Row 83 [RS]: K4, p18, C2B, p6, k4.
All even rows 84–102 [WS]: K4, knit the knit sts and any bobble sts and purl the purl sts to last 4 sts, k4.
Row 85: K4, p16, C4B, p6, k4.
Row 87: K4, p15, C3B, p8, k4.
Row 89: K4, p13, C4B, p9, k4.
Row 91: K4, p12, C3B, p11, k4.
Row 93: K4, p10, C4B, p12, k4.
Row 95: K4, p8, MB, C3B, p14, k4.
Row 97: K4, p7, MB, C3B, p15, k4.
Row 99: K4, p6, C4BMB, p16, k4.
Row 101: K4, p5, T2B, k1, p18, k4.

Continue work following this sequence: *Leaf on Right, Vine Winding Left, Leaf on Left, Vine Winding Right; repeat from * once; then Leaf on Right once. Finish by working Vine Winding Left through Row 49. Place sts on stitch holder. Repeat all steps for Scarf Side 2.

Block both scarf sides. Weave together using the following instructions. Take sts off holder and place on a needle with the needle's point at the beginning of the row. Work with both right sides

PATTERN

Scarf Side 1

With larger needles, cast on 33 sts.
Rows 1–14: Work Lace Chart.
Row 15 [RS]: K4, purl to last 4 sts, k4.
Row 16: K16, m1, k17. 34 sts.

of the scarf on the outside, needles parallel, needlepoints side by side. On the back needle, cut a yard and a half of yarn and thread with a tapestry needle (TN). Run TN through the first stitch on the front needle as if to knit and leave on the needle. Next, run TN through the first stitch on the back needle as if to purl and leave on the needle. Working yarn should stay below the needles. From now on, work two stitches on the front needle followed by two stitches on the back needle each time.

Step 1: On the front needle (FN), run TN through first stitch as if to purl and pull stitch off FN (P & off). Run TN through the second stitch of FN as if to knit and leave it on the needle (K & leave). Gently tighten the yarn as you go, taking care not to pull too tight so as not to form a ridge.

Step 2: On the back needle (BN) you will do just the opposite. Run TN through the first stitch as if to knit and pull stitch off BN (K & off). Run TN through the second stitch of BN as if to purl and leave it on the needle (P & leave).

Repeat steps 1 & 2 until you reach the vine knit stitch. Here we transition to knitting. On FN, rather than knit & leave, purl & leave this st. On BN, knit & off and then knit & leave the vine stitch. Next, FN: K & off, p & leave. BN: P & off, k & leave. Now, we have to switch back to purling. FN: K & off, k & leave. BN: P & off, p & leave. Repeat steps 1 & 2 through the end of the row.

Hood
Left side
Using larger needles, cast on 53 sts. Work in reverse st st for 3.75"/9.5cm, ending with a WS row. Dec 1 st at beg of next row [RS] and every foll 4th row 3 times more. 49 sts. Work 1 WS row even. Dec 1 st at beg of next row [RS] and every 2nd row 18 times more. 30 sts. Work 1 WS row even. Bind off 2 sts at beg of next row [RS] and every 2nd row 2 times more. 24 sts. Bind off rem sts.

Right side
Using larger needles, cast on 53 sts. Work in reverse st st for 3.75"/9.5cm, ending with a RS row. Dec 1 st at beg of next row [WS] and every foll 4th row 3 times more. 49 sts. Work 1 RS row even. Dec 1 st at beg of next row [WS] and every 2nd row 18 times more. 30 sts. Work 1 RS row even. Bind off 2 sts at beg of next row [WS] and every 2nd row 2 times more. 24 sts. Bind off rem sts.

FINISHING

Block hood pieces to 10"/25.5cm across the bottom and 11.5"/29cm tall. Sew hood sides together. Re-block hood using a small, round form such as a child's soccer ball. Using smaller needles, with RS facing, pick up and knit 75 sts evenly across hood bottom. This will produce a slight gather. Work k1, p1 ribbing for 1"/2.5cm. Bind off in rib. Weave in ends. Align top center seam of the hood with center of scarf & pin. Sew scarf to hood along the underside of scarf edging and enjoy!

ABOUT THE DESIGNER

Knitting is meditation as far as Jenny is concerned. After a lifetime of knitting other people's patterns, she loves the process of making an idea come to fruition.

Jenny's website is daydreamerknits.com and her Ravelry ID is jennyw.

http://daydreamerknits.com
jennyw on Ravelry.com

SPANISH STEPPES

BY JILL WRIGHT

INTERMEDIATE

This interesting stepped scarf was inspired by a visit to a small Spanish village. It had very narrow streets and long, winding stairways lined with fabulous hanging baskets and vines. The stepped design causes the scarf to appear to slant when worn.

FINISHED MEASUREMENTS

Width: 8"/20.5cm
Length: 70"/178cm

MATERIALS

Green Eyed Monsters Silkling [70% merino wool, 30% silk; 360yd/330m per 100g skein]; color Poppies; 2 skeins

1 set US #7/4.5mm straight needles

Cable needle (cn)
Row counter (optional but very helpful)

GAUGE

22 sts/30 rows = 4"/10cm in stockinette, unblocked

STITCH INSTRUCTIONS

Lace 1 (panel of 8 sts)
Row 1 [RS]: (Yo, k2tog, k2) twice.
Rows 2: Purl.
Row 3: (K2, yo, k2tog) twice.
Row 4: Purl.
Rep Rows 1–4.

Lace 2 (panel of 8 sts)
Row 1 [RS]: Slip 2 to cn and hold to back, k2, k2 from cn; slip 2 to cn and hold to front, k2, k2 from cn.
Row 2 and all WS rows: Purl.
Rows 3, 5, 7: Knit.
Row 9: Rep Row 1.
Row 11: K1, (ssk, yo) 3 times, k1.
Row 13: K1, (yo, k2tog) 3 times, k1.
Row 15: Rep Row 11.
Row 16: Purl.
Rep Rows 1–16.

Lace 3 (panel of 8 sts)
Row 1 [RS]: P1, k6, p1.
Row 2: K1, p6, k1.
Row 3: P1, yo, ssk, k2, k2tog, yo, p1.
Row 4: Rep Row 2.
Row 5: P1, k1, yo, ssk, k2tog, yo, k1, p1.
Row 6: Rep Row 1.
Rep Rows 1–6.

PATTERN NOTES

Scarf is bordered by 3-st panels of garter stitch. Lace panels are separated by 6-st panels of garter st. When casting on in the middle of work, use the backward loop or cable method.

CHARTS

LACE 1

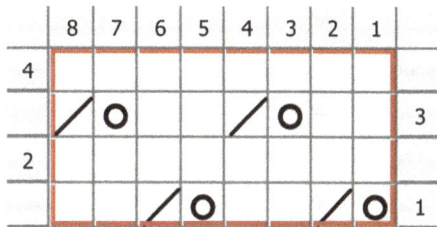

LACE 2

8	7	6	5	4	3	2	1	
								16
	O	\	O	\	O	\		15
								14
	/	O	/	O	/	O		13
								12
	O	\	O	\	O	\		11
								10
	\	⌐	⋀	¬	/			9
								8
								7
								6
								5
								4
								3
								2
\	⌐	⋀	¬	⋀	¬	/		1

LACE 3

8	7	6	5	4	3	2	1	
●							●	6
●		O	\	/	O		●	5
●							●	4
●	O	/			\	O	●	3
●							●	2
●							●	1

PATTERN

Cast on 42 sts. Knit 6 rows.

Step 1
*Row 1 [RS]: K3, work Lace 1, k6, work Lace 2, k6, work Lace 3, k3.
Row 2 [WS]: K3, work Lace 3, k6, work Lace 2, k6, work Lace 1, k3.
Continue as established by Rows 1–2 for a further 58 rows.†
Next row [RS]: K17, work Lace 2, k6, work Lace 3, k3.
Next row [WS]: K3, work Lace 3, k6, work Lace 2, k17.
Rep the last 2 rows once more.
Next row: Bind off 14 sts, k until there are 3 sts on RH needle, work Lace 2 over 8 sts, k6, work Lace 3 over 8 sts, k3, cast on 14 sts. 42 sts.

Step 2
Row 1 [WS]: K17, Lace 3, k6, Lace 2, k3.
Row 2 [RS]: K3, Lace 2, k6, Lace 3, k17.
Row 3: Rep Row 1.
Row 4: K3, Lace 2, k6, Lace 3, k6, Lace 1, k3.
Row 5: K3, Lace 1, k6, Lace 3, k6, Lace 2, k3.
Continue as established by Rows 4–5 for a further 58 rows.
Next row [RS]: K17, Lace 3, k6, Lace 1, k3.
Next row: K3, Lace 1, k6, Lace 3, k17.
Rep the last 2 rows once more.
Next row: Bind off 14 sts, knit until there are 3 sts on RH needle, Lace 3, k6, Lace 1, k3, cast on 14 sts. 42 sts.

Step 3
Row 1 [WS]: K17, Lace 1, k6, Lace 3, k3.
Row 2 [RS]: K3, Lace 3, k6, Lace 1, k17.
Row 3: Rep Row 1.
Row 4: K3, Lace 3, k6, Lace 1, k6, Lace 2, k3.
Row 5: K3, Lace 2, k6, Lace 1, k6, Lace 3, k3.
Continue as established by Rows 4–5 for a further 58 rows.
Next row [RS]: K17, Lace 1, k6, Lace 2, k3.
Next row [WS]: K3, Lace 3, k6, Lace 1, k17.
Rep the last 2 rows once more.
Next row: Bind off 14 sts, knit until there are 3 sts on RH needle, Lace 1, k6, Lace 2, k3, cast on 14 sts. 42 sts.

Beginning of Step 4
Row 1 [WS]: K17, Lace 2, k6, Lace 1, k3.
Row 2 [RS]: K3, Lace 1, k6, Lace 2, k17.
Row 3: Rep Row 1.**

Rep from * to ** once more, then from * to † once.
Knit 6 rows.
Bind off.

FINISHING

Weave in ends. Block each step to 8"/20.5cm wide by 10"/25.5cm long, with 3"/7.5cm wide steps along the bound-off/cast-on edges.

ABOUT THE DESIGNER

Jill Wright is a crochet and knitwear designer who originally comes from Newcastle, England. She's an avid yarnaholic and multi-crafter. On Ravelry she's known as Woolcrafter.

http://www.woolcrafting.com
Woolcrafter on Ravelry.com

SCHEMATIC

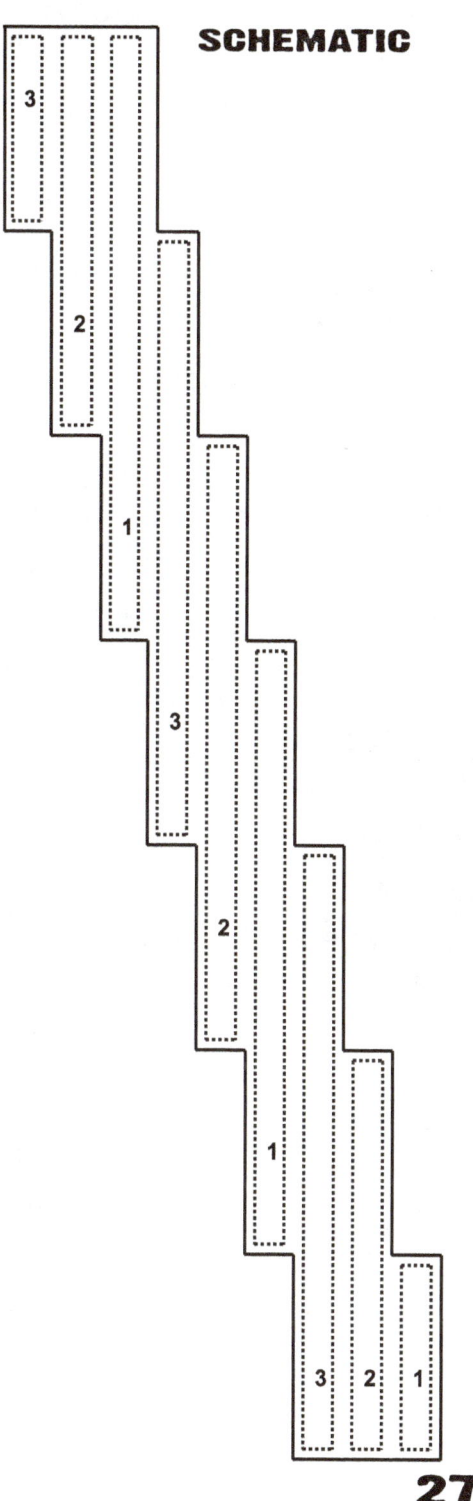

TOSSED LEAVES SCARF

BY MARGARETE DOLFF

EXPERIENCED

For a long time I had in mind a scarf made of different shapes of leaves, in different shades of green, with different yarns to resemble the abundance of colors, golden lights, and stormy weather of my favorite season, autumn.

Wanted: A country style scarf, looking like randomly tossed leaves, wrapped around the shoulders.

Now it is a recipe. Make it your own. Take the shapes and play with size, color, yarn, assembling your one-of-a-kind-scarf/stole/cowl/shawl.

FINISHED MEASUREMENTS

Length: About 84"/214cm
Width varies according to placement of leaves: 6–11"/15–28cm

MATERIALS

[MC] Aade Long Artistic [100% Pure New Wool; 440 yd/400m per 100g]; color: green; about 150g (skeins are of varying sizes)

[CC 1–6] Around 80yds/70m each of 6 contrast colors, approximately worsted weight (or hold together 2 strands of thinner yarn). The yarns used in the sample are discontinued, from the designer's stash; they include 4 shades of Rowan Rowanspun 4 Ply (used double stranded) and 2 shades of Rowan Yorkshire Tweed 4 Ply. Grab a bowl and fill it with an irresistible mix of colors and yarns from your stash! Working one leaf at a time, this might be a great project for knitting on the go.

Set of 2 US #3/3mm double pointed needles, or appropriate size to get desired drape

Removable stitch markers
Regular stitch markers
Design board or table to lay out motifs
Pins, needle and thread for basting

GAUGE

Gauge is not crucial for this pattern. Most of the leaves shown were worked with an approximate gauge of 20 sts/26 rows = 4"/10cm, slightly felted.

STITCH INSTRUCTIONS

I-cord: *Knit across all sts on needle. Do not turn at end of row, but slide work back to other end of needle, draw yarn tightly across back of work; repeat from *.

PATTERN

Oval Leaf With Serrated Edges (make 18 with MC, varying shape and size as desired according to notes below)
Cast on 4 sts. Work I-cord for 4 to 12 rows for stem.

Begin leaf:
Row 1 [RS]: K2, m1, k2. 5 sts.
Rows 2, 4, 6, 8, 10, 12 [WS]: Sl1 pwise, purl to last st, sl1 pwise.
Row 3: (K1, m1) 4 times, k1. 9 sts.
Row 5: K2, (m1, k1) 6 times, k1. 15 sts.
Row 7: K3, m1, knit and place removable m in next st, m1, k3, m1, knit and place removable m in next st, m1, k3, m1, knit and place removable m in next st, m1, k3. 21 sts.
Row 9: (Knit to marked st, m1, k marked st, m1) three times, knit to end. 27 sts.
Rows 11 and 13: Rep Row 9. 39 sts.
Row 14 [WS]: Bind off 4 sts, purl to last st, sl1 pwise. 35 sts.
Row 15: Bind off 4 sts, (knit to marked st, m1, k marked st, m1) three times, knit to end. 37 sts.
Rows 16: Rep Row 2.
Remove the 2 outside markers, leaving only the center marker.
Row 17: Knit to marked st, m1, k marked st, m1, knit to end. 39 sts.
Row 18: Rep Row 2.
Row 19: Bind off 4 sts, knit to marked st, m1, k marked st, m1, knit to end. 37 sts.
Row 20: Bind off 4 sts, purl to last st, sl1 pwise. 33 sts.
Rows 21–28: Rep Rows 17–20. 25 sts.
Continue in stockinette, bind off 4 sts at beg of next 4 rows, then

bind off 3 sts at beg of next 2 rows. 3 sts. P3tog and fasten off. Weave in ends.

Variations:

For a wider base and larger leaf:

Repeat Row 9 another time before beginning bind offs (45 sts) and stop working the center "vein" increases when 23 sts rem. Bind off 4 sts at beg of every row until 7 sts remain, then bind off 2 sts at beg of next 2 rows. Finish with sl1, k2tog, pass slipped stitch over.

For a wider base and a more heart-shaped leaf:
After starting the bind offs, keep increasing at all 3 markers on RS rows as long as possible.

For a smaller elongated leaf:
After Row 13, remove the outside markers and increase around the center marker only.

Make a shorter, rounder leaf by stopping the center vein increases sooner.

Make a larger elongated leaf by continuing the center vein increases as long as possible.

Pointed Leaf With Three Veins
(make 25 in different colors)

With CC, cast on 8 sts.
Base:
Row 1 [RS]: Knit.
Rows 2, 4, 6, 10, 12, 14, 16, 18 [WS]: Sl1 pwise, purl to last st, sl1 pwise.
Row 3: K2, M1L, pm, k2, M1L, pm, M1R, k2, pm, M1R, k2. 12 sts.
Row 5: (Knit to marker, M1L, sl marker) twice, (M1R, knit to marker, sl marker) twice, knit to end. 4 sts inc'd.
Rows 7, 9, 11, 13, 15, 17: Rep Row 5. 40 sts.
Row 19 [RS]: Bind off 4 sts, (knit to marker, M1L, sl marker) twice, (M1R, knit to marker, sl marker) twice, knit to end. 40 sts.
Row 20 [WS]: Bind off 4 sts, purl to last st, sl1 pwise. 36 sts.

First Point

Row 1 [RS]: SSK, k7, sl1, turn leaving rem sts unworked. 9 sts.
Row 2 [WS]: P2tog, purl to last st, sl1 pwise. 8 sts.
Row 3: SSK, knit to last st, sl1 pwise. 7 sts.
Rep Rows 2–3 until 3 sts rem. P3tog. 1 st. Do not fasten off. Turn to RS. With LH needle, pick up 4 sts from slipped sts on left side edge of point. (K1, pass 1st st on RH needle over 2nd st) four times, m1 in

corner, pass 1st st over 2nd. 1 st on RH needle. Knit across all sts. 27 sts.
Second Point

K17, SSK, k7, sl1. 26 sts. Turn.
Row 1 [WS]: P2tog, p6, sl1 pwise. Turn leaving rem sts unworked. 8 sts.
Row 2 [RS]: SSK, knit to last st, sl1 pwise. 7 sts.
Row 3: P2tog, purl to last st, sl1 pwise. 6 sts.
Rep Rows 2–3 until 3 sts rem. P3tog. 1 st. Do not fasten off and do not turn. With LH needle, pick up 4 sts from slipped sts on right side edge of point. (K1, pass 1st st on RH needle over 2nd st) four times, m1 in corner, pass 1st st over 2nd. 1 st on RH needle. Purl across all sts. 18 sts.

Center Point

Row 1 [RS]: SSK, knit to last st, sl1 pwise. 17 sts.
Row 2 [WS]: P2tog, purl to last st, sl1 pwise.
Rep Rows 1–2 until 3 sts rem. P3tog and fasten off.

To vary the size:

Make the first bind offs (Rows 19–20) 5 sts instead of 4, leaving 34 sts instead of 36. Work the first and second points over 10 sts each as given and make the center point 16 sts wide instead of 18. Or, work another increase row and start working the points with 40 sts, varying the size of the points again.

FINISHING

For a more country style look, gently wash and felt your leaves.

Carefully block each leaf.

On a design board or table arrange and rearrange your leaves until you like the look.

Step aside and look again at your scarf.
If some areas don't "feel" right, try again. Reposition leaves until you are satisfied.

Tossed leaves are arranged around one larger oval leaf in the center, with two rather straight strips of leaves sewn to it at an angle. With the center on one shoulder, both ends can easily be drapes and fastened with a striking pin.

Baste leaves in place. On wrong side of scarf, carefully whipstitch any overlapping part of leaf to the leaf below. This is essential. It is the backbone of your scarf and defines its strength.

On the right side, inconspicuously tack any loose flaps to the leaf below. Block again to desired shape.

Make it your own:

With contrasting yarn embroider veins on some leaves. Think of caterpillars, beetles, butterflies, berries, chestnuts, rose hips. The sky is the limit.
Use pearls, beads, wood, crystal, buttons, charms, embroidery thread, whatever suits the style of your project, to elaborate your idea.

ABOUT THE DESIGNER

Margarete Dolff has finally found the time to enjoy her love of playing with color, fiber, shapes and technique. When it comes to knitting and designing, she knows all about sock frenzy and has a soft spot for the plus sized and the tall.

http://www.maz-wolldesign.de
maz on Ravelry.com

DIAMOND SAMPLER

BY SYLVIA CANNIZZARO

INTERMEDIATE

An introduction to traditional Estonian lace stitches in a smaller project with nontraditional construction. The scarf is worked from the center, alternating sides with increasing complexity, and ending with a simple lace edge. No grafting is required.

FINISHED MEASUREMENTS

Width: 13"/33cm
Length: 72"/183cm

MATERIALS

Sanguine Gryphon Gaia Lace [60% silk, 40% cashmere; 420yd/384m per 50g skein]; color Cobblestone Mazes; 2 skeins

1 set US #2/2.75mm straight needles

Stitch markers
Stitch holders
Waste yarn
Crochet hook for provisional cast on

GAUGE

18 sts/32 rows = 4"/10cm in stockinette, blocked

CHARTS

Charts 1–6 begin on page 36.

PATTERN NOTES

The scarf is worked outward from the center, from two balls of yarn, alternating ends. Charts 5 and 6 are worked on both halves. See page 35 for a construction diagram.

Note that only RS rows are shown on the charts. All WS rows are purled, with a border of 5 garter stitches at each side. Be sure to work the last WS row after each chart.

PATTERN

Using the crochet provisional method (see Shaker Moebius, p. 13), cast on 61 sts.
Row 1: Knit.
Rows 2–4: Sl1 pwise, knit to end.

Chart 1
Row 1: Sl1 pwise, knit to end.
Row 2: Sl1 pwise, k4, purl to last 5 sts, k5.
Row 3: Sl1 pwise, k4, work Chart patt to last 5 sts, k5.
Row 4: Sl1 pwise, k4, purl to last 5 sts, k5.
Continue as set by Rows 3–4 until you have worked the 16 rows of Chart three times.
Next row [RS]: Sl1 pwise, knit to end.
Next row: Sl1 pwise, k4, purl to last 5 sts, k5.
Next row: Sl1 pwise, knit to end increasing 1 st. 62 sts.
Knit 3 rows, slipping the first st of each row as est. Place sts on holder.

Remove the waste yarn from the provisional cast on and place the live sts on the needles with WS facing. Join second ball of yarn. Knit 1 row. 61 sts.

Chart 2
Row 1 [RS]: Sl1 pwise, knit to end.
Row 2 [WS]: Sl1 pwise, k4, purl to last k sts, k5.
Row 3: Sl1 pwise, k4, work Chart patt to last 5 sts, k5.
Row 4: Sl1 pwise, k4, purl to last 5 sts, k5.
Continuing as set by Rows 3–4, work Chart Rows 1–26 once, then Chart Rows 1–28 once.
Next row [RS]: Sl1 pwise, knit to end.
Next row: Sl1 pwise, k4, purl to last 5 sts, k5.
Knit 4 rows, slipping the first st of each row as est. Place sts on holder.

Return to other end of scarf. Transfer sts from holder to needles. 62 sts.

Chart 3
Row 1 [RS]: Sl1 pwise, knit to end.
Row 2 [WS]: Sl1 pwise, k4, purl to last k sts, k5.
Row 3: Sl1 pwise, k4, work Chart patt to last 5 sts, k5.
Row 4: Sl1 pwise, k4, purl to last 5 sts, k5.
Continue as set by Rows 3-4 until you have worked the 18 rows of Chart three times.
Next row [RS]: Sl1 pwise, knit to end.
Next row: Sl1 pwise, k4, purl to last 5 sts, k5.
Next row: Sl1 pwise, knit to end decreasing 1 st. 61 sts.
Knit 3 rows, slipping the first st of each row as est. Place sts on holder.

Return to other end of scarf. Transfer sts from holder to needles. 61 sts.

Chart 4
Row 1 [RS]: Sl1 pwise, knit to end.
Row 2 [WS]: Sl1 pwise, k4, purl to last k sts, k5.
Row 3: Sl1 pwise, k4, work Chart patt to last 5 sts, k5.
Row 4: Sl1 pwise, k4, purl to last 5 sts, k5.
Continue as set by Rows 3-4 until you have worked the 24 rows of Chart three times.
Next row [RS]: Sl1 pwise, knit to end.
Next row: Sl1 pwise, k4, purl to last 5 sts, k5.
Knit 4 rows, slipping the first st of each row as est.

Chart 5
Row 1 [RS]: Sl1 pwise, knit to end.
Row 2 [WS]: Sl1 pwise, k4, purl to last k sts, k5.
Row 3: Sl1 pwise, k4, work Chart patt to last 5 sts, k5.
Row 4: Sl1 pwise, k4, purl to last 5 sts, k5.
Continue as set by Rows 3-4 until you have completed the 72 rows of Chart.
Next row [RS]: Sl1 pwise, knit to end.
Next row: Sl1 pwise, k4, purl to last 5 sts, k5.
Next row [RS]: Sl1 pwise, knit to end increasing 4 sts evenly spaced. 65 sts.
Knit 7 rows, slipping the first st of each row as est. Place sts on holder.

Return to opposite end of scarf and work Chart 5 as for other side.

Chart 6
Row 1 [RS]: Sl1 pwise, knit to end.
Row 2 [WS]: Sl1 pwise, k4, purl to last k sts, k5.
Row 3: Sl1 pwise, k4, work Chart patt to last 5 sts, k5.
Row 4: Sl1 pwise, k4, purl to last 5 sts, k5.
Continue as set by Rows 3-4 until you have completed the 32 rows of Chart.
Next row [RS]: Sl1 pwise, knit to end.
Next row: Sl1 pwise, k4, purl to last 5 sts, k5.
Knit 7 rows, slipping the first st of each row as est.
Next row: Sl1 pwise, knit to end decreasing 6 sts evenly spaced. 59 sts.

Edging
Row 1 [RS]: Sl1 pwise, knit to end.
Row 2 [WS]: Sl1 pwise, purl to last st, k1.
Row 3: Sl1 pwise, *k1, yo, k2, sl1, k2tog, psso, k2, yo; rep from * to last 2 sts, k2.
Rep Rows 2-3 seven times more, then Row 2 once more.
Bind off all sts using a double strand of yarn as foll: K1, *k1, return 2 sts from RH needle to LH needle, k2tog tbl; rep from * until all sts are bound off.

Return to other end of scarf and work Chart 6, Edging, and bind off as for first end.

FINISHING

Soak scarf in lukewarm water. Gently press the water out, then roll in a towel to remove excess water. Block the scarf to desired measurements, and allow to dry completely.

ABOUT THE DESIGNER

Sylvia Cannizzaro, Sligo on Ravelry, lives in the Northeast Kingdom of Vermont. Experimenting with knitting styles, patterns, and techniques gets her through the long winters. She blogs at Sligo's Muse.

http://sligosmuse.blogspot.com
sligo on Ravelry.com

SCHEMATIC

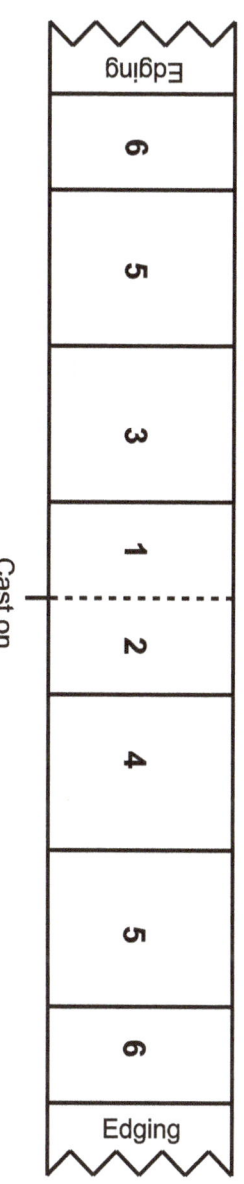

CHARTS FOLLOW...

CHART 1

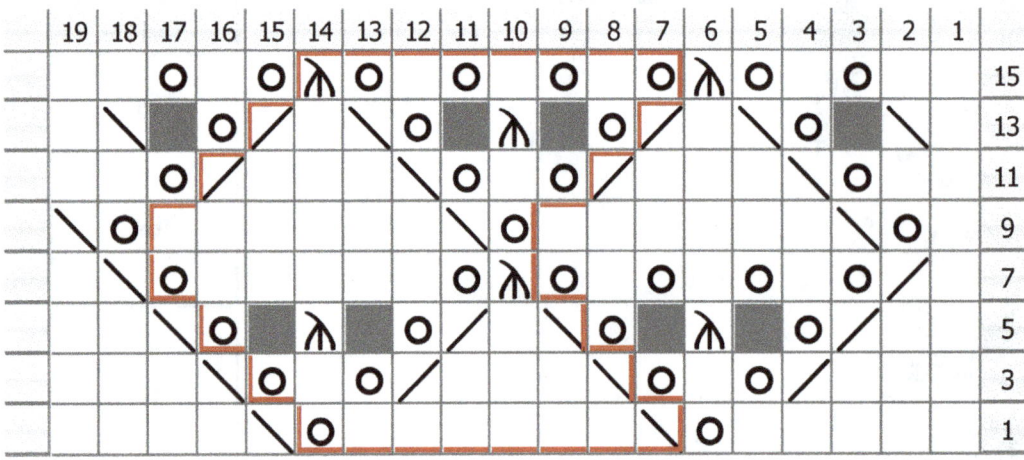

CHART 2

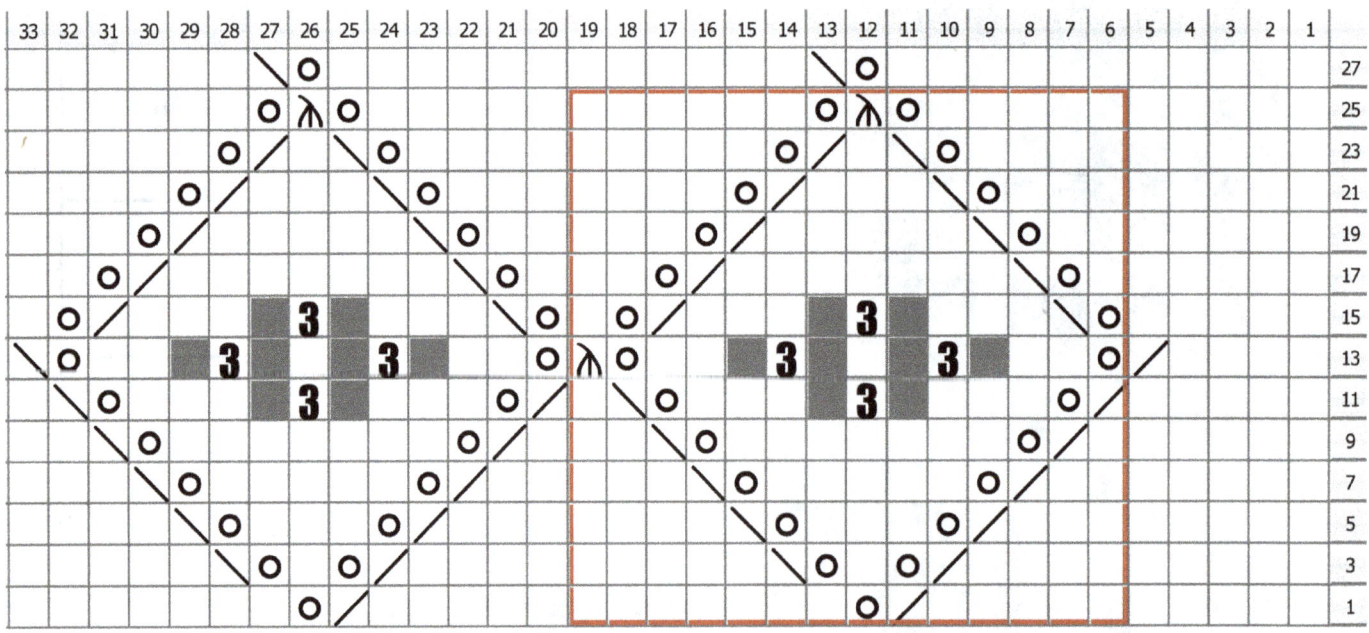

CHART 3

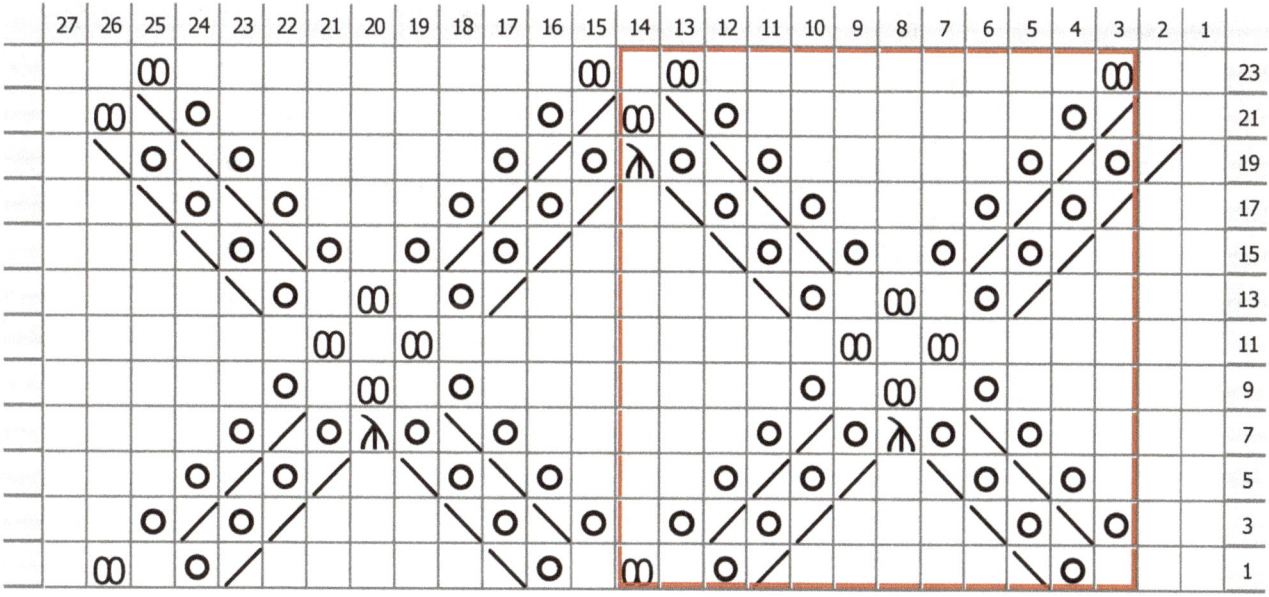

CHART 4

CHART 5

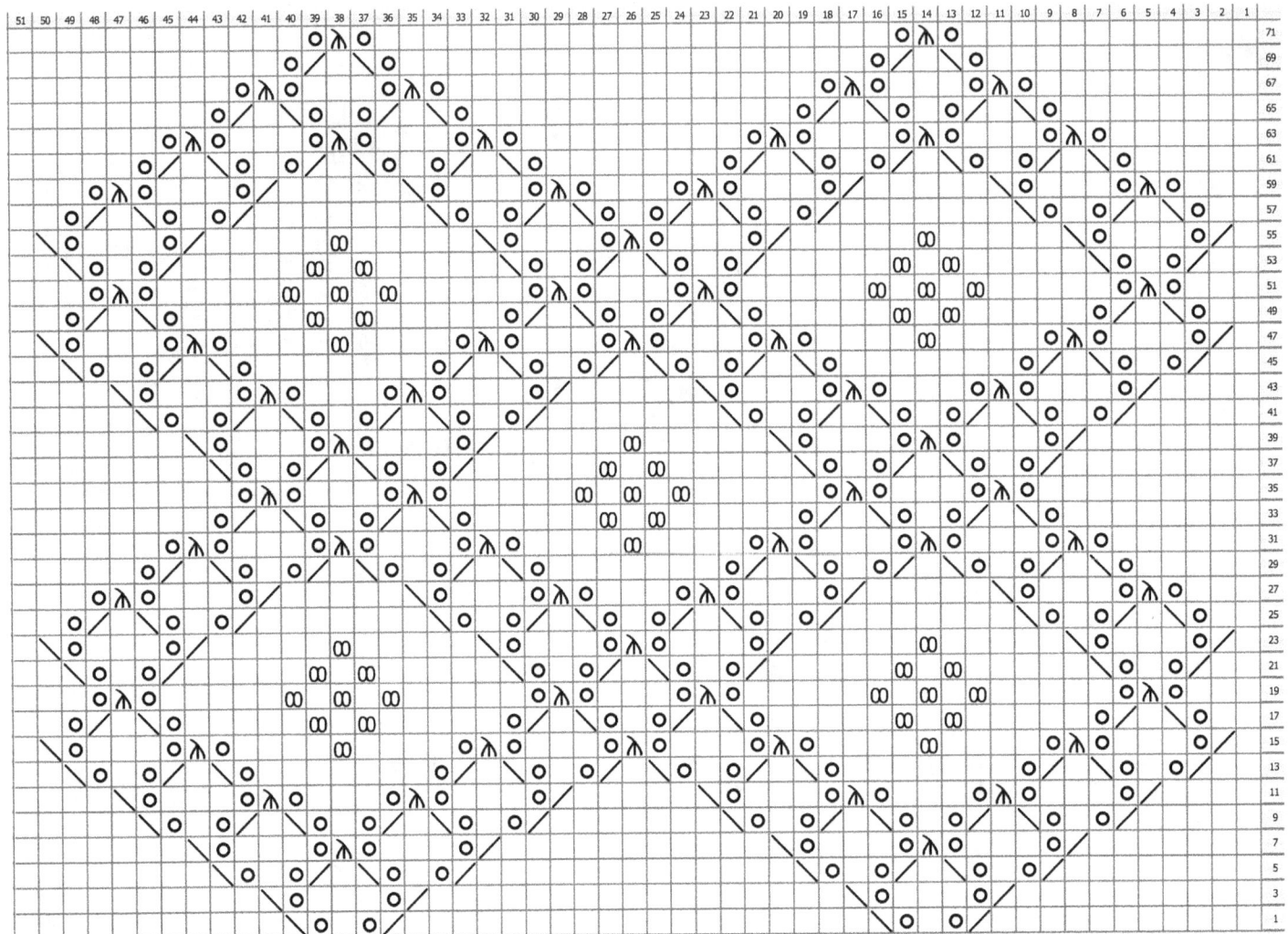

CHART 6

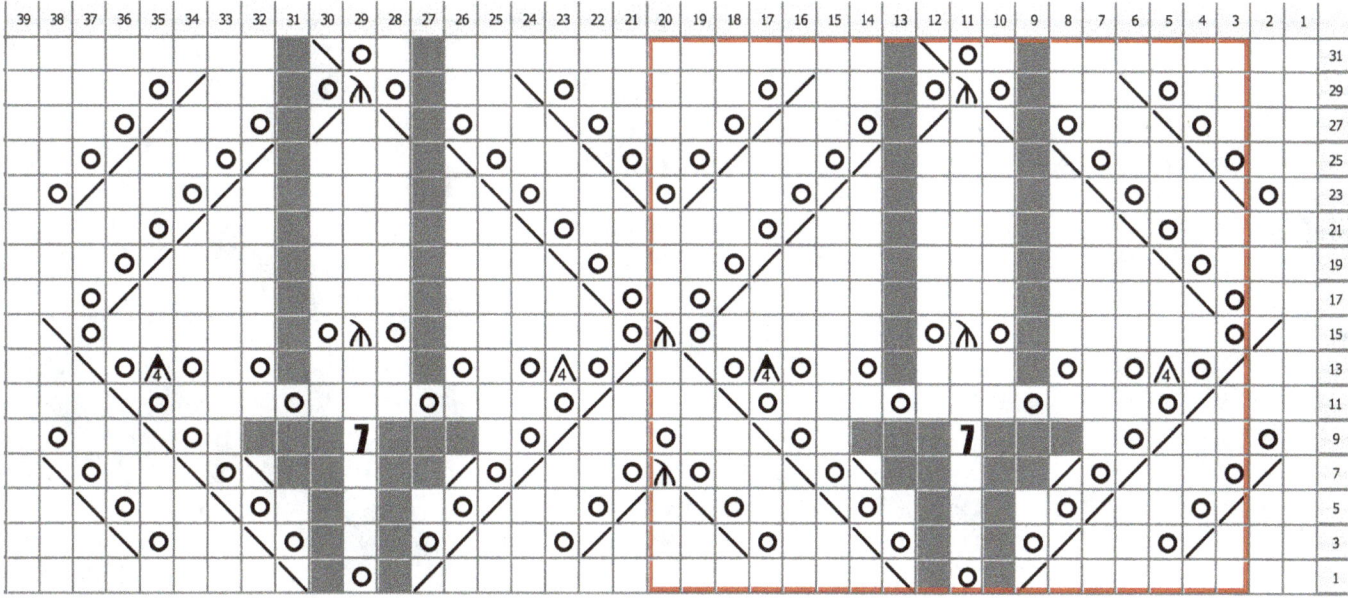

LAINEET
BY VALERIA KERKKÄ

EASY

The Laineet scarf was designed with both hand-dyed and hand-spun yarns in mind. The stitch pattern combines a herringbone pattern with slipped stitches, and is a great for displaying the best features of colorful yarns.

FINISHED MEASUREMENTS

Width: 8.25"/21cm
Length: 60"/152cm

MATERIALS

Indigodragonfly Merino Silk Single [60% merino, 40% silk; 500yd/457m per 225g skein]; color Vancouver Melt; 1 skein

1 set US #8/5mm straight needles

Waste yarn
Crochet hook for provisional cast on

GAUGE

20 sts/26 rows = 4"/10cm in stockinette

PATTERN NOTES

The scarf is a rectangle, knit from end to end. It uses needles slightly larger than recommended by the yarn manufacturer because the slip stitch pattern is denser than stockinette stitch.

PATTERN

Using crochet provisional cast on (see Shaker Moebius, p. 13), cast on 50 sts.
Row 1 [WS]: With MC, purl.

Row 2: Sl1, (p1, k1) twice, (sl1, k1, psso but do not drop st off LH needle, k into back of the st, drop st off needle) twice, k1, *wyif sl3, k1, (sl1, k1, psso but do not drop st from LH needle, k into back of the st, drop st off needle) twice, k1; repeat from * three times more, (p1, k1) twice.

Row 3: Sl1, k1, p1, k1, (p2tog, but do not drop these stitches off LH needle, purl into the first of these stitches again, drop both stitches off needle) three times, *k3, (p2tog, but do not drop these stitches off LH needle, purl into the first of these stitches again, drop both stitches off needle) three times; repeat from * three times more, (k1, p1) twice.

Repeat Rows 2 and 3 until the scarf measures 60"/152cm. Bind off. Remove waste yarn from provisional cast on, place live sts on needle, re-join yarn and bind off.

FINISHING

Block gently to spread out the patterning, and weave in ends.

ABOUT THE DESIGNER

Valeria Kerkkä has been knitting for most of her life. Her design inspiration comes from nature, architecture and movements of every day life.

nettlefly on Ravelry.com

ACKNOWLEDGMENTS

Thank you to the designers who created such beautiful work for the book. Our biggest thanks to photographer Robert Gladys, makeup artist Elle Gemma, and to our models Arabella Proffer, Rachel Harner, Susan Prahst and Terra Incognita, as well as to Abra Forman, whose considerable talents helped bring the project together in its early stages. Sarah Jo Burch helped keep things running so Abra and Shannon could get things done, and MJ Kim did a massive amount of organizational work before we handed everything off to the talented technical editor, Alexandra Virgiel. Elizabeth Green Musselman came late to the team but helped enormously with wrapping up loose ends.

The book wouldn't be nearly as beautiful without the yarns contributed by the companies below.

We'd also like to thank the generous patrons whose Kickstarter support helped make this book series possible.

YARNS FEATURED IN THIS BOOK:

Indigodragonfly (http://indigodragonfly.wordpress.com)
Natural Born Dyers (http://www.naturalborndyers.com)
Berroco (http://berroco.com)
Yarn Love (http://www.shopyarnlove.com)
Kangaroo Dyer (http://www.kangaroodyer.com)
Alpaca With A Twist (http://www.alpacawithatwist.com)
Green Eyed Monsters (http://www.greeneyedmonsters.co.uk)
Aade Long (http://www.hot.ee/yarns/tooted_en.html)
The Sanguine Gryphon has split into two companies since this book was commissioned: (http://verdantgryphon.com) and (http://cephalopodyarns.com)

ABOUT COOPERATIVE PRESS

partners in publishing

Cooperative Press (formerly anezka media) was founded in 2007 by Shannon Okey, a voracious reader as well as writer and editor, who had been doing freelance acquisitions work, introducing authors with projects she believed in to editors at various publishers.

Although working with traditional publishers can be very rewarding, there are some books that fly under their radar. They're too avant-garde, or the marketing department doesn't know how to sell them, or they don't think they'll sell 50,000 copies in a year.

5,000 or 50,000. Does the book matter to that 5,000? Then it should be published.

In 2009, Cooperative Press changed its named to reflect the relationships we have developed with authors working on books. We work together to put out the best quality books we can, and share in the proceeds accordingly.

Thank you for supporting independent publishers and authors.

We're on Ravelry as CooperativePress. Please join our low-volume mailing list and check out our other books at...

HTTP://WWW.COOPERATIVEPRESS.COM

ABOUT FRESH DESIGNS

Shannon Okey wanted to do something to showcase emerging design talent after she left the editorship of a UK print knitting magazine; Fresh Designs is the result. A partnership between talented designers and primarily small/indie yarn companies (all of whom are thanked on the previous page — please help support these remarkable companies when you next shop for yarn), the first 10 Fresh Designs books have also broken the mold for designer compensation. Each time you purchase a Fresh Designs book or pattern, the designers receive a royalty share. We hope you'll enjoy meeting the designers in these pages, and that you'll check out the other books in the Fresh Designs series.

ABBREVIATIONS

alt	alternate
approx	approximately
beg	begin/beginning
CC	contrasting color
cn	cable needle
dec	decrease(s)/decreasing
dpn	double pointed needle
est	established
foll	follows/following
inc	increase(s)/increasing
k	knit
k2tog	knit 2 together
kfb	knit into the front and back of the same stitch
kwise	knitwise
LH	left hand
m1	make 1 stitch
MC	main color
p	purl
patt	pattern
pm	place marker
p2tog	purl 2 together
psso	pass slipped st over
pwise	purlwise
rem	remain/remaining
rep(s)	repeat(s)
RH	right hand
rnd(s)	round(s)
sl	slip
ssk	slip, slip, knit these 2 sts together
tbl	through the back loop
tog	together
WS	wrong side
wyib	with yarn in back
wyif	with yarn in front
yo	yarn over

CHART SYMBOLS USED

knit
RS: knit stitch
WS: purl stitch

c2 over 2 left
RS: sl 2 to CN, hold in front. k2, k2 from CN
WS: none defined

c2 over 2 right
RS: sl2 to CN, hold in back. k2, k2 from CN
WS: none defined

Left Twist
RS: sl1 to CN, hold in front. k1, k1 from CN
WS: Left Twist

c2 over 1 right
RS: sl1 to CN, hold in back. k2, k1 from CN
WS: sl1 to CN, hold in back. k2, k1 from CN

Right Twist
RS: Skip the first stitch, knit into 2nd stitch, then knit skipped stitch. Slip both stitches from needle together OR k2tog leaving sts on LH needle, then k first st again, sl both sts off needle.
WS: Skip first stitch, and purl the 2nd stitch, then purl the skipped stitch. Slip both sts from needle together.

c2 over 1 left
RS: sl2 to CN, hold in front. k1, k2 from CN
WS: sl2 to CN, hold in front. k1, k2 from CN

c2 over 1 right P
RS: sl1 to CN, hold in back. k2, p1 from CN
WS: sl1 to CN, hold in back. k2, p1 from CN

3-to-7
RS: Working in the next 3 sts tog, (k1, yo, k1, yo, k1, yo, k1).
WS:

k 2tog special
RS: k2tog, do not slip off needle; knit the same 2 tog again tbl, slip off needle.
WS:

k3tog
RS: Knit three stitches together as one
WS: Purl three stitches together as one

nupp
RS: In next st, loosely (k1, yo, k1, yo, k1, yo, k1); on following WS row, purl these 7 sts tog

ssssk
RS: (Sl 1 kwise) 4 times, insert LH needle into the backs of these 4 sts and knit them tog
WS:

c2 over 1 left P
RS: sl2 to CN, hold in front. p1, k2 from CN
WS: sl2 to CN, hold in front. p1, k2 from CN

 k3tog special
RS: k3tog, do not slip off needle; yo, knit the same 3 sts tog again, slip off needle
WS:

sl1 k2tog psso
RS: slip 1, k2tog, pass slip stitch over k2tog
WS: none defined

k2tog
RS: Knit two stitches together as one stitch
WS: Purl 2 stitches together

ssk
RS: Slip one stitch as if to knit, Slip another stitch as if to knit. Insert left-hand needle into front of these 2 stitches and knit them together
WS: Purl two stitches together in back loops, inserting needle from the left, behind and into the backs of the 2nd & 1st stitches in that order

yo
RS: Yarn Over
WS: Yarn Over

make one left
RS: Place a firm backward loop over the right needle, so that the yarn end goes towards the front
WS: Place a firm backward loop over the right needle, so that the yarn end goes towards the back

make one right
RS: Place a firm backward loop over the right needle, so that the yarn end goes towards the back
WS: Place a firm backward loop over the right needle, so that the yarn end goes towards the front

make one
RS: Make one by lifting strand in between stitch just worked and the next stitch, knit into back of this thread.
WS: Make one by lifting strand in between stitch just worked and the next stitch, purl into back of this thread.

No Stitch
RS: Placeholder - No stitch made.
WS: none defined

knit tbl
RS: Knit stitch through back loop
WS: Purl stitch through back loop

slip wyif
RS: Slip stitch as if to purl, with yarn in front
WS: Slip stitch as if to purl, with yarn in back

 purl
RS: purl stitch
WS: knit stitch

47

www.ingramcontent.com/pod-product-compliance
Lightning Source LLC
Chambersburg PA
CBHW081917180426
43199CB00036B/2822